MICHEAL OSMOND

UNTOLD FACTS ABOUT WEALTH CREATION

Wealth creation is a goal that many people aspire to but few actually accomplish. Why would that be? All things considered, I think the response is basic the vast majority don't have a substantial arrangement or system for abundance creation. They either don't have the foggiest idea where to begin or they don't have any idea how to support the energy.

For quite a long time individuals have been attempting to comprehend the mystery of abundance creation, some have contended that it's just a question of difficult work and assurance

While others have guaranteed that there is a sure outlook that prompts abundance creation. So what's the reality of the situation, is there confidential to abundance creation?

Yes, there are ways to make money, but there isn't a single secret; rather, a combination of factors determines a person's ability to make money. One of the most significant circumstances is Mentality.

 Abundance creation requires a specific outlook, people who are fruitful in making abundance have a particular perspective about cash and abundance they view abundance as something made, not as something acquired or coincidentally found. They know that hard work, dedication, and a willingness to take risks are the keys to wealth. A great many people never become rich since they just have some unacceptable outlook, they accept that abundance is something that you either have or don't have and that it's difficult to make abundance on the off chance that you don't as of now have it. This couldn't possibly be more off-base anybody can become affluent assuming they're willing to fix their mentality and really buckle down. to become rich you want to begin having a similar outlook as a well off individual, you really want to trust that it's workable for you to

make accomplishment
for you and you want
to make a move.

To get it going you can
have the best outlook
on the planet however
without activity nothing
will occur. You likewise

should face challenges, many individuals stay trapped in their usual ranges of familiarity yet nothing extraordinary at any point comes from that, in the event that you're not able to face challenges accomplish nothing perfect. So what move would it be advisable for you to make? There's no right response as the best strategy will fluctuate contingent upon your exceptional conditions however there are a few general rules that can assist with directing you.

The initial step is you want to get clear on what you need. What precisely would you like to focus on. Characterize your objective, get it on paper and read it consistently. Your mind is strong enough to figure out a way to almost any goal you give it. The mind is always devising a strategy to achieve a goal when it has a strong, burning desire for it, which brings us to the Second Step.

 Make an arrangement. record what it would take to accomplish your objective, separate it into little advances and start by dealing with venturing out even a little activity is superior to no activity. It starts the method involved with making energy, it's urgent to have persistence and adhere to your arrangement in the event that you're going for the gold achievement. Rome wasn't underlying a day nor is extraordinary riches. Such countless individuals need to get rich rapidly they need to find that one mysterious equation that will make them a tycoon short-term yet truly this isn't the truth of how a great many people Make Monetary progress.

Abundance creation takes time, discipline and concentration if you need to be rich, you should show restraint, you should invest the long stretches of energy expected to construct something of significant worth really at that time will you see the sort of results that affluent individuals have accomplished.

One more suggestion you could hear frequently with regards

to abundance creation is to foster different floods of pay. The majority of people only have one source of income, which is their job. As a result, their wealth is tied to how much time they spend at work. However, what if there was a way to diversify your income so that you have multiple streams that don't need your time? This wouldn't just make you richer yet would likewise give you significantly more opportunity. So how might you make different surges of pay?

There are numerous ways however probably the most well-known remember money management for stocks, land , digital currencies ,beginning a side business, outsourcing or making an item that you can sell. Anything course you choose to take, recollect that abundance creation is an excursion not an objective. By making little strides and reliably adding to your revenue stream you can accomplish Independence from the rat race and fabricate the existence you need.

Now, there are a few important reasons to have multiple sources of income.

In the first place, it assists with enhancing your pay and safeguard you from Monetary shocks. Assuming one stream of pay evaporates you will in any case have others to return to.

Second, it can assist you with developing your abundance all the more rapidly. Having different surges of pay offers you the chance to reinvest and compound your abundance all the more really. Elon Musk is a genuine illustration of somebody who has various floods of pay he has Tesla SpaceX neuralink and SolarCity and he is likewise a financial backer in various different organizations. Presently certain individuals center exclusively around getting more cash however more cash is just the outcome, if you need to be really well off you want to zero in on the most effective ways you can offer some incentive for other people, again Elon

Musk is an ideal illustration of this he didn't become Rich by zeroing in on getting more cash he became well off by distinguishing better approaches to make esteem he began organizations that reformed Transportation energy money and space investigation he made items that impacted the world to improve things.

  If you have any desire to become rich, you want to track down better approaches to make esteem you really want to track down new issues to settle, new business sectors to take advantage of and better approaches to serve others. At the point when you do, you'll be well headed to monetary overflow.

 Presently, suppose you have the right mentality, an

arrangement to make a move on, and various types of revenue. You accomplish the abundance and the objectives, you set the monetary test sorting out some way to maintain and develop your riches. The most important thing here is to put your money into things that will go up in value over time. This could be anything from stocks and cryptocurrencies to real estate. Billionaires typically have a diversified portfolio that helps them protect their wealth in the event that the market goes down. Moreover, tycoons frequently have serious areas of strength for an of associations and persuasive individuals. Having a high worth Organization can be significant with regards to making and keeping up with your progress.

At last tycoons normally have a

positive outlook and are continuously searching for ways of working on themselves and their organizations. They stay ahead of the curve because they are always learning and developing. Thus, there you have it the key to abundance creation start carrying out this guidance today and you will be well en route to making the abundance you want.

9 798853 188167